HOME OFFICES
& STUDIES

HOME OFFICES
& STUDIES

● ●

A PRACTICAL GUIDE TO DESIGN AND DECOR

DENISE BROCK

MEREHURST

First published in 1998 by Merehurst Limited,
Ferry House, 51-57 Lacy Road, Putney, London SW15 1PR

Copyright © Merehurst Limited 1998

ISBN 1 85391 736 2

A catalogue record of this book is available from
the British Library

Edited by Cally Law
Designed by Sue Miller
Special photography by Lucinda Symons
Styled by Denise Brock
Illustrated by King and King
CEO & Publisher: Anne Wilson
International Sales Director: Mark Newman
Colour separation by Bright Arts (HK) Ltd
Printed in Singapore by Tien Wah Press (Pte) Ltd

PUBLISHER'S NOTE

Standard measurements for the width of MDF board vary from
country to country. If you cannot find materials with the exact
measurement quoted in the project, we suggest you purchase
materials with the nearest dimensions available.

ACKNOWLEDGEMENTS

The publishers wish to thank the following photographers and
organizations for their kind permission to reproduce the
photographs in this book on the following pages:
4 above Ray Main; 4 below left James Merrell / Options / Robert
Harding Syndication; 7 James Merrell / Options / Robert Harding
Syndication; 9 Neues Wohnen / Camera Press; 11 Paul Ryan
(designer: Maeve Morgin) International Interiors; 13 Ducal
Furniture; 14 J&I Kurtz / Camera Press; 15 Schoner Wohnen /
Camera Press; 16 Paul Ryan (designer: Ellie Dylan) / International
Interiors; 17 Andrew Cameron / Homes and Ideas / Robert Harding
Syndication; 18 -19 Paul Ryan (designer: Sasha Waddell) /
International Interiors; 21 Elizabeth Whiting and Associates; 23
Schoner Wohnen / Camera Press; 25 Simon Upton / Options /
Robert Harding Syndication; 26 Nadia Mckenzie / Ideal Home /
Robert Harding Syndication; 27 Paul Ryan (designer: Wolfgang Joop) /
International Interiors; 29-31 only David Loftus / Ikea Room

Contents

Introduction

Working from home, whether occasionally or full-time, has become part of many people's lives. Personal computers make it possible by being quick and efficient – while good, modern communications keep you in touch. You may need a home office only now and again if your work load cannot be contained within the usual working day, or full-time if you are running a business from home. Even just for paying household bills or for playing on the computer for fun, a desk, a chair and some storage are essential.

The essence of a comfortable and efficient office is a well-designed space with a good choice of furniture and an agreeable colour scheme. There is no need to recreate the look of a starchy formal office. You can have fun with colour and style and give the space a relaxed feel – even if you work from home all day, everyday. Choose a style that suits you, whether it is country and traditional or modern and sleek. There are colours that are best for working, but always go for something that makes you feel happy.

Neatness and good organization are essential, as there is often little space to spare in the home and you will feel better and work more efficiently in orderly and agreeable surroundings. Good storage is paramount, so that everything in your working life is close at hand and exactly where it should be. Shelving is the main provider of storage and, with cupboards, filing cabinets, boxes and files, will solve all your storage problems. Deciding on the best arrangement is the key to a successful home office and you will need to give some thought to how you work and what you need around you. Comfort and safety are also important, and a well-designed desk of the right size and height – with a comfortable chair – is essential to avoid repetitive strain injury.

Plan ahead and you can create a stylish office that will make home working both effective and enjoyable.

Right: Metal filing cabinet stripped back to its basic glory looks stylish and is useful too.

Chapter one

Setting up at home

Why do you need a study or home office? Is it just for occasional use or will you be spending many hours in it? Either way, your home office should, above all else, be functional.

In it, you should be able to get on with your work easily and safely. The room should also be comfortable, so that writing, typing and paperwork become more inviting activities. If not, they will be easy to put off. Storage for stationery and equipment should be close at hand and easy to find, making good organization a priority. This may simply mean putting envelopes in one drawer, paper in another and pens in a convenient box on the desk top.

Planning is vital to make the space work. The size of the desk and the type of storage and equipment you choose will vary according to the amount and the type of work you need them for. So, before you start buying any furniture or deciding where it will go, think about what you will do in your study, who will use it and how frequently it will be used.

What is the space used for?

Working from home can mean many things. It can mean spending an occasional quiet hour sorting out work papers and writing cheques for household bills, or more creative pursuits such as sewing or perfecting a craft. At the other extreme, your home could be your business base – where you earn your living.

All homes need an office of sorts, even if it is just a table top and a pocket file to keep the bills and household accounts tidy and up to date. But, as a personal computer becomes an essential item in many homes, a place needs to be found that is large enough to house it.

With sophisticated office equipment, it is possible to work from home without feeling you are too far away from the cut and thrust of things. Faxes, phones, copiers and computers keep you in touch with the world of work. These items are smaller than ever and can be incorporated into a reasonably compact area to create a complete and efficient work space. Those arduous journeys to and from the office are a thing of the past.

Who will use it?

The work space may be for the exclusive use of one person – their own special area where everything can be placed and planned for their specific work or activities. If it is not a business space, then it may be for two people to share – in which case, the layout and furniture need to suit both of them. This may mean that both a computer desk and an area for craft activities are needed. A large table that can be cleared would suit more than one purpose provided there is somewhere to put the cleared items. For a family, the space will have to be more adaptable, to suit all ages and sizes. Chair seats need to be adjustable and surfaces hardwearing.

How much furniture or storage is needed?

As space is often a luxury, keep the furniture down to a bare minimum. A desk or large table is essential for all home work and some sort of storage for papers and equipment will be needed nearby. Add a

Right: Tools need to be close at hand in a work area. Here they hang on hooks from a peg rail, leaving the worktop clear for the project in hand.

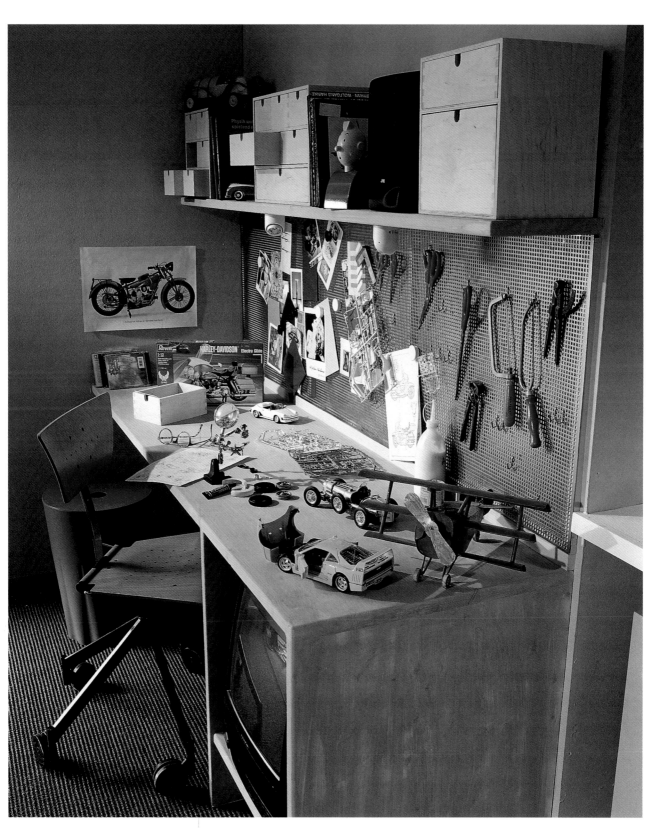

comfortable office chair and you are all set. Think about what you plan to use. There may be books and boxfiles or small items in cartons, correspondence in soft folders or a filing cabinet. You will need to decide how best they can be stored. How much equipment will you need? A phone, fax, computer and possibly a photocopier may be necessary. Some of these may be placed on the desk – or another surface could be called into service. Small equipment could be mounted on the wall to save surface space.

Make a comprehensive list of all the items you will need to store, from files to stationery. Also list all the equipment you require, so that you have a clear idea of the space needed to house it all.

Where can you put it?

If you are lucky, you may have a spare room that could become a study. If not, there may be a room that could serve a dual purpose. A bedroom, for instance, is not much used during the day and part of it could become an office and so extend its usefulness. As you may not find it relaxing to have a reminder of your work at the foot of the bed, you will need to find a way to hide the desk area at the end of the day.

Adding a work zone to a dining room makes good use of the

How much space should you allocate to the study?

The amount of space you allocate to your study depends on how much time you will spend there and the type of work you will do in it. If your work requires you to be in your office a lot, a large space may make your day-to-day life more pleasant. Alternatively, if your work involves travelling or visiting clients, a small comfortable area may be sufficient.

Some jobs require a large amount of equipment, files and reference material, while other work requires very little apart from communications equipment and a computer. If you use a PC just for surfing the Internet, playing games and writing letters, you will not need much room. On the other hand, sewing and creative activities require a lot of space for handling materials, ironing and storage. A large table and plenty of storage space may demand a separate room. Consider how you will use your work space before deciding whether it should be separate or shared.

available space. Here, again, you will need a method of disguising the inevitable work clutter when you have a dinner party. This could be done with a screen – or the entire work space could be concealed behind doors.

Look for a room or space that is conducive to concentration. It will need to be quiet, preferably away from any street noise. If it is tucked away at a far corner of the house, other members of the family can get on with their lives without bothering you and without you irritating them with constant requests for quiet. However, there is no point in choosing a spot that is cold and uncomfortable – which may be the case with a hallway or loft conversion.

If you receive work visitors, the room will need to be near the front door so that you do not have people traipsing through the whole house. Personal clutter need only be cleared from the limited part they see, in the work area. One good point about this is that you will have an invisible line of demarcation between home and work zones.

Once you have decided on a room or area in which to work, it is a good idea to place the desk next to a window. Good daylight is essential for designers and it generally makes working more enjoyable for everyone.

Chapter two
Planning your space

It can be tempting to rush into decorating a room without thinking it through. Perhaps you have seen one particular piece of furniture that you like and feel you must have. Before you choose anything, it pays to take time to plan your new room so that you make the best of the opportunity. Decide how you will arrange the furniture and choose the colour scheme and type of lighting, and you will have a better overall room. Your special piece of furniture may well be perfect – but in a smaller version or a different shape. By planning ahead you avoid compromising a successful room scheme through an impulse buy.

Below: In this office different areas have been defined for different types of work. Storage and administration are done at the far end with an adjustable desk next to the window for telephone calls. Two people can work together here quite comfortably.

11

Making a floor plan

In a study, every spare inch of space is vital for storage, furniture or equipment, so make a plan of the room and decide on the best arrangement.

Use graph paper to draw out a scaled version of the room or available space. Cut pieces of paper to represent furniture you would like to put into the room. Although this takes time, it means you can plan the best layout with accuracy.

The desk is best placed near a window to take advantage of natural light, which should ideally come from the side. The minimum you will need to add is shelving, a filing cabinet and a chair. You may also need a surface for a printer or fax machine.

The pieces of equipment that you use most frequently are best kept close to the desk. So, if you are constantly looking at files, the filing cabinet should be nearby, while shelves for equipment could be further away.

Note where power points are positioned when deciding on the site for equipment. You may need to have extra power points added before you decorate.

Space to move

If your work involves spreading out books, samples and papers, it is a good idea to aim for the

How to make space in a shared room

Sometimes the only solution is for a work space to be part of another room in the house. This is likely to be a restricted area so good planning and concealing ideas need to be called upon to make the space functional and attractive. Look for a natural break in the room and take advantage of it, such as the small part of an L-shaped room or an alcove. The space under the stairs or on the landing may be called into use as an office. Ideally look for a spot with a window and enough headroom to be comfortable, but also one that can be disguised or screened off in someway. This could be done just by using a set of shelves or a freestanding screen.

largest desk you can. Try this in your plan in the first instance, then gradually reduce its size to make way for other items. If possible, add a smaller table to make an L-shaped work surface.

A good depth for a desk is about 75 cm (29 in). Any deeper and the items on the far side will not be readily accessible.

Once you have put all your pieces of furniture in the space, you will need to allow room in front and around certain items to make them practical. A distance of 1 m (39 in) should be allowed in front of a desk so that

you can get in and out of your chair. Also allow 1 m (39 in) in front of a filing cabinet to pull out the drawers and have access to the contents.

Do not pack in so many items of furniture that the space feels cramped and oppressive. If you need more storage, use the height of the walls, either for tall cupboards or for shelves – but remember, you will need to be able to reach the top ones without climbing on furniture below. For visual balance, keep the heights of the items compatible. A couple of two-drawer filing cabinets will double as a surface for a printer or fax.

Advantages of a separate room

A separate room, even if it is a small utility room or tiny box bedroom, will allow you to dedicate the space to a work environment. This will offer the best setting for concentration. The layout of the room can be arranged exclusively for work and designed specifically for your purpose. If necessary, it can be filled to capacity with specific storage, shelves and equipment. You also have the luxury of being able to leave work set up at the end of the day without it interfering with the other activities of the home (although this may not always be best work practice). You can simply close the door on it.

Dining room

As we live more casual lives nowadays, a separate dining room is often used just for entertaining. Without daily use it becomes under employed and would be ideal to double as a study. If it is a completely separate room, the door can be closed to give you a quiet and private space in which to work. If you need the office just for writing letters and bills you may be able to use the dining table as a desk, with all your stationery stored in a cupboard close by. But if you use a computer it is best to put it on a desk so that the keyboard is at the right height and the computer itself does not need to be moved. An alcove beside a fireplace or a corner would be a good starting point. Built-in furniture would make the best use of the space. Shelves built up as high as possible will provide storage for books and stationery.

The desk will need to be about 60 cm to 75 cm (24 in to 30 in) deep, which is deeper than most alcoves. A fixed surface to this depth is ideal if space permits; a fold-out arrangement is also a good idea and will look neat when not in use. If there is a second alcove, shelving here would create a balanced look and be useful for display.

For occasional use, one of the dining chairs could become the desk chair; for frequent use, a good, neat office chair is best. The idea is to integrate the two functions in a homely way so that the office part does not jar and look unfriendly.

Chapter three

Which room to share?

Spare rooms are not always on offer in smaller homes and so the decision has to be: which room to share as a home office? If the office is for occasional use only, it does not really warrant a dedicated room. Decide which of your rooms is least employed. Do you need a dining room to be exclusively a dining room all year round when it is only used on high days and holidays? Is there a space in your living room that is used to house a piece of furniture that is not serving a useful purpose? You may find a corner that would lend itself to becoming a small work area. By adding a home office you will be doubling the usefulness of the room and making a special and efficient work space.

Above: Understairs space can be transformed into an efficient office. Furniture of different heights and widths can be chosen to fit the space exactly.

13

Living room

A living room is not an ideal room to double as a study. It is frequently used by the rest of the household and you will need to clear away all your paperwork at the end of the day. However, while you work in it as your office it will be comfortable and relaxing, which is likely to add to your productivity rather than diminish it. You will be surrounded by favourite objects and have the opportunity to put your feet up occasionally.

As in the dining room, an alcove site is a good idea. An L-shaped room may offer a good spot, tucked away from the general space. A bay window provides a good source of natural light and a defined work area.

You will need to be especially well-organized and tidy if you work in a living room. The style of desk and storage will have to match that of the overall room. A computer and fax machine should be discretely placed; hidden if possible. Place decorative objects in the work space so it integrates with the rest of the room. Use attractive files for paperwork and, if possible, have built-in furniture with doors to hide office paraphernalia.

Bedroom

A bedroom is generally unused during the day and you might feel it is a good choice. The

Landing

A tiny, tucked-away corner on a landing can be made into a useful study. With some thought, a wasted area can become a personal retreat perfect for letter-writing and studying. A built-in desk may be the answer here, to make the most of every last centimetre. Otherwise, a bureau would look good, perhaps with shelves above. If you feel there is not enough space for a chair, use a folding one and hang it on the wall when not in use.

drawback is that you might not feel comfortable surrounded by work while you try to relax at the end of the day. Make a clear divide between the two areas. A screen of some sort will hide the desk and create a separating feature. It can be a solid folding screen or a curtain suspended from the ceiling. You may be able to position furniture so that it separates the two zones. Place your desk, for instance, so that you face away from the bed. Another good idea is to face a

Left: An unused space on a landing can become an efficient office. The desk spans the landing, next to the natural light, with neatly arranged shelves along the wall behind.

Right: A neat, built-in desk is surrounded by ample storage and has good lighting to make it an ideal work place within a bedroom.

window, so that as you sit at the desk you feel in a separate place.

A spare bedroom is a different story. Here, a bed can be replaced with a sofa bed or futon. Day-to-day, the room will look like a study, and when guests visit, it can be easily transformed into a bedroom.

Understairs

The space under the stairs is an excellent spot for a study. The width under the stairs is often just right for a desk and storage. Shelving could fill where the stairs are highest, with a desk below and a small filing cabinet at the lowest corner.

Power points for equipment and lighting should be close at hand, so you may need new ones fitted. A good source of overall light is important as there may not be much available from a natural source. Spotlights are a good idea as well as a desk lamp. A lamp that clips onto a shelf will give you more desk space.

Chapter four

How to conceal your home office

It is a good idea wherever possible to make some visible divide between the office space and the main function of the room. This is especially important in a living room or bedroom, where you will also want to relax. The screen will hide the office equipment and furniture so that you are not constantly reminded of the troubles of the day.

Behind a screen

The easiest way to create a divide between the two areas is to use a folding screen. When you have finished for the day, this can be pulled across the work area to hide the desk and the clutter that can easily accumulate on it. The least expensive screens can be bought in kit form. They are made of MDF and can be finished with a couple of coats of paint or a layer of fabric. Little castors will make them move more easily.

In a cupboard

A deep alcove or the space under the stairs could be closed off completely with folding doors. Hinged narrow doors will fold open when you use the office.

Colour and neatness

Keep everything simple and be scrupulously neat to make an office area less obvious. A pale colour used through the entire room will make the areas meld together. You need to have files and boxes in the same colour and put everything away when not in use.

Furniture positions

The position of furniture may help create an enclosed and separate feeling. For example, a bookcase could be positioned at right angles to the wall, facing into the office area. The back would need to be covered with wood to look good, or perhaps two bookcases could be placed back to back.

Soft line

The dividing feature need not be solid. A panel of fabric hung from a wire would make a visual break and is easily drawn aside as necessary. In a plain white or a bold-coloured fabric, and threaded through eyelets, it would have a modern look. A wide blind in fabric, wood or cane could be fixed to the ceiling to section off an area.

With lighting

Lighting can be a clever and subtle way to make a division. The simplest way is to have two separate lighting arrangements – one for the general area and one for the office area. You can then choose to focus on the space you are using, leaving the rest of the room in shadow. Dimmers will add to the control you have in each area.

Plants

Position a large plant next to your desk so that it is partially hidden. In this case, extreme neatness will help the desk blend into the main area.

Above: An all-white scheme and orderly shelves help make this modern office area blend with the adjoining kitchen. The long shelves give a sleek look and contain the boxes and files perfectly.

Right: A tiny alcove has shelves fitted right up to the top to make good use of all available space. Care has been taken to make sure both the keyboard and computer screen are at the correct height for working.

Chapter five

Decorating and colour

A lthough it may seem difficult with so much equipment, a home office should blend in and become an integral part of the home. There is no point in transporting all the austere qualities of a real office to your home. It should be both comfortable and stimulating, so that you enjoy your surroundings while working, and the space should be decorated so that you can work efficiently.

How to blend the office with the style of the room or house

Despite the need to create an efficient work area, the decor of your office should blend into the overall look of the room or house. If the office shares space in another room, there should be one general scheme – with the colours and furnishing in each area linking strongly to give a unified look. A modern desk would appear out of place in a traditional room, so opt for a wooden desk to match other wooden pieces in the room and keep equipment in cupboards or under cover when not in use. Do not, however, forfeit good lighting and a comfortable seat and desk for style. Your comfort and well being are paramount.

Traditional office

A traditional scheme relies on a good wooden desk and furniture. The warmth of the wood will be the starting point and the effect should be rich and cosy. Although it is possible to find antique desks and chairs, be careful to check the desk height and the amount of support that a chair gives. If you will be sitting all day, you may want to consider something contemporary with a period style. There are several furniture ranges that look traditional but are the correct height and size for lengthy use. They also have special features to accommodate the latest computer technology. For comfort, you might like to consider buying a reproduction chair to use with an old desk. Compare the shades of the woods and measure up before you commit yourself, to be sure they are compatible.

Decoration should be as simple as possible. Patterned walls and

Right: A handsome, dark wooden desk with a traditional chair and desk lamp sit in a dramatic 1930s-style living room. The roll top will hide away everything when not in use.

curtains may make the room seem too fussy. Warm colours such as mustard, cream or terracotta tone with dark wood and give one overall shade that is traditional too.

Keep the window treatments simple. A wooden Venetian blind or a roller blind will look neat. If you want curtains, choose plain, light ones, hanging from a pole.

Country style

An office can be created in any style. The fresh, outdoors look of a seaside chalet in crisp white and blue will bring a refreshing atmosphere to a work room or office. Simplify furnishing with a trestle table for a desk and open shelves for storage. Wood-clad walls and bare floorboards can be painted white to set the scene. Add blue-and-white striped blinds and keep the accessories light or white.

A pretty country scheme will be relaxing to work in. It relies on an informal arrangement of pine furniture, old and new, perhaps painted pieces too, with a touch of floral fabric at the window just to lift the room. A large pine cupboard or shelved wardrobe could be pressed into service as a stationery store. A mix of tables and cupboards will contribute to the casual country air but choose pieces that will be fully useful, so that you do not end up with clutter. Scrubbed

Modern offices

A modern scheme suits an office very well as surfaces and colours can be sleek and practical, in metal, wood and melamine. Plain, light colours, or bold and bright ones, set off modern furniture to good effect. Solid colour used on walls gives an air of orderliness and calm to counterbalance the stress of working life and the clutter that accumulates on work desks.

Gentle off-white or pastel colours will be soothing; pale green in particular has a calming effect. Bright colours can be stimulating, so add them in small areas, such as on files or a noticeboard. Pale colours used overall on walls, windows and flooring give a sleek look that will set off attractive furniture and help make a small room seem larger. However, if your furniture is less than perfect, bold colours will distract the eye and give an interesting scheme. Use toning colours together, such as soft shades of blue and green or green and yellow, to create a calming effect.

wooden floorboards or sisal rugs are practical floorings. Add decorative pieces sparingly.

Effect of colour

Colour has a strong effect on the appearance of a room and the mood of the people using it.

Generally, warm colours have an advancing quality, making

Right: A pretty Scandinavian-style room in a simple scheme of powder blue, white and red is both an office and guest room. Shelves with decorative trim have a work surface below and a spacious cupboard alongside.

the room seem smaller and warmer, whereas cold colours such as blue or green retreat and make the space seem larger and cooler. You will need to bear this in mind if a room is cold or dark. Small rooms benefit from light, subtle colours.

Colours for an office are often neutral creams and off-whites, as these will make a space seem larger and will not distract you from your work. White can sometimes be too clinical. However, if you are working with colours all day, whether sewing or colour matching, white will be a good overall scheme. Pale greens and blues are soothing and refreshing, and so may be a good choice if you work under a lot of stress.

Bright, warm colours such as red, orange and yellow can be stimulating, but working in a red room may make you irritable. Confine these colours to small areas only.

Yellow is a sunny, welcoming colour which in soft shades makes a cheerful room that will lift the spirits.

Chapter six
Choosing furniture and equipment

The furniture you choose should make your office efficient and attractive. It will obviously need to fit the available space and make the best of it. Special thought should be given to the desk and chair, as they should be comfortable enough for the amount of time you spend there. Equipment too should be carefully considered for its function, size and usefulness before you make an investment.

Built-in or freestanding desk?

A built-in desk will make good use of all available space and can be any size you like. If you have an alcove, a surface can be fitted into it on battens attached to the side and back walls, then you can buy a small chest of drawers to stand underneath.

A well-designed freestanding desk will have handy drawers, with possibly a filing drawer, and will be the correct height. Choose a size to suit any work you like to spread out and also think about the equipment that will be standing on it. Various wood finishes as well as plain paint colours are available to suit your scheme. If you choose an old desk, try out a chair with it first to check whether it fits comfortably underneath. The height may be unsuitable for using a computer, but fine for writing a diary.

Shelves

Walls offer a convenient storage solution as they can be covered in shelves. Store little-used items on high shelves while everyday items should be lower down. A small set of steps would help you reach higher shelves.

Desk: height and size

A comfortable desk height is about 65 cm (26 in) to 76 cm (30 in). The depth of a desk can vary from 50 cm (20 in) up to 80 cm (32 in). The width of the desk will depend on what kind of work you do. If you need to lay out lots of work, go for the biggest one the room can accommodate. If you just use a phone and a computer, a small desk may be the answer.

Chair: comfort and support

If you use your desk only for writing letters or paying bills, a dining chair or stool will be sufficient – and these are easier to match with other chairs in the room. For prolonged work, an adjustable office chair is essential to prevent back pains. Swivel office chairs are available in various colours to match your room scheme.

Storage

Good and plentiful storage is essential. An ideal arrangement would consist of open shelves, cupboards and filing cabinets. The final combination depends on your personal needs. Shelves should be strong enough for large quantities of papers and books. Freestanding shelves are inexpensive, so extras can be bought as and when you need them, if space permits.

Cupboards can be fitted with extra shelves to hold stationery supplies, files or craft materials, while filing cabinets are the best solution if your work means frequent access to files. For infrequent access, box files or ring-binder files kept on shelves will keep papers neatly stored. Remember, if you start storing files and books on the floor, something is wrong. Perhaps you can throw some files away or find space for a new shelf.

Computer desks

These are designed to house all the components of a computer, often with a sliding keyboard drawer that can be pushed out

Right: A mixture of freestanding and fitted furniture is the best arrangement in a home office. The fitted furniture will make the most of available space while freestanding pieces look light and homely.

of sight when not in use. More importantly, they are designed so that the screen and keyboard are at the right height – when your fingers are on the keyboard, your forearms should be at right angles to the upper arms. Your feet should be flat on the floor – if not, use a footrest.

Comfortable chair or sofa for breaks

It is good to take breaks from the desk. A comfortable chair or sofa makes a welcome change for checking documents. A small armchair is ideal where space is short, perhaps with a lamp nearby.

Accessories

A noticeboard with the week's activities clearly displayed will keep you well informed and your thoughts clear. Putting often-used items in small boxes will help keep a desk top tidy. Pencil pots and a box for disks, cards and paper clips will keep stationery close at hand. Letterheads and envelopes can be kept within easy reach in a small drawer file. A small trolley can house your stationery and be wheeled across the room.

Mod cons

Telephones, faxes and computers are essential parts of home office life. Look for machines that combine functions, such as a fax/answerphone/telephone.

Many functions can be run from a computer. To make more work-top space, a telephone can be mounted on the wall and the computer screen placed on a wall-hung shelf.

23

Chapter seven

Storage

A good storage system will help you work more efficiently and feel in control of your working days. If you know exactly where all your files and information are kept, you will be able to act more quickly and keep calm at busy times. In addition, your office will look attractive and orderly and be a pleasant place in which to work, either everyday or just once in a while.

Storage to suit your needs

As a starting point, draw up a list of all the items you will use and store in your office. You may find this list divides into different types of item, such as books, magazines, files, stationery, craft materials, large pieces of equipment and machinery, samples and so on. Now you can calculate roughly how much and what type of space you need. You may decide on boxfiles or a filing cabinet for paper references; boxes for magazines; shelf space for books; a small table for a fax or printer and a cupboard for materials, stationery or samples.

Shelves, cupboards and filing cabinets

Open shelves are the most useful and adaptable type of storage. They will hold books, paperwork, files and boxes with ease. Fitted shelves make the best use of space. They can fill the full height of the wall and be made to any length. Longer shelves may sag unless you make sure they have plenty of support, either from lengths of batten fixed along the back wall or from a series of brackets. Choose a strong material for the shelves themselves such as MDF board or solid wood. Freestanding shelving units can be an inexpensive choice and can be moved to another room if necessary or taken with you when you move home. Always allow for extra shelf space as it is sure to be filled.

If you have lots of small items to store, they can be put into separate boxes placed inside a cupboard. Label each box clearly so you know exactly what is inside, and you have the start of a successful system. Cupboards are more expensive than shelving but, with some attractive doors and good proportions, a cupboard can be an eyecatching focal point as well as hiding away a lot of items.

You could balance your outlay by investing in a good cupboard and economizing by buying cheap shelving. If space is tight, be sure that you have room to open the cupboard doors and stand in front of it.

An inexpensive idea is to fit an old wardrobe with shelves. Remove the hanging rail and fit battens on either side and the back of the interior to support shelves. In this way you can place them at heights to suit what you want to put inside.

Filing cabinets are essential if you have a lot of paperwork such as correspondence, agreements and plans that you refer to frequently. Before you start filling your cabinet, decide whether you work mostly by name, date or subject, so the files are arranged and labelled in the most useful way. Secondhand metal filing cabinets are fairly easy to find and can be sprayed or painted to match your room. Four-drawer cabinets hold plenty and use little floor space, while one- or two-drawer versions can double up as low-level storage and a surface for a piece of equipment.

Right: Large paper-covered storage boxes are labelled and decorated with black-and-white photo prints to make a strong visual impression. A custom-made screen separates the area from the rest of the room.

Above: Shelving will solve most storage problems, holding books and magazines, trays and labelled boxes of small items, so that everything can be seen and quickly found.

On display or hidden away?

All possessions can be divided roughly into two groups. They are either worthy of putting on show or should be hidden away. If you find something attractive then put it out on open shelves. It could be an everyday item, such as a pot of pens or colour-ful labels – whatever you like. Plus, of course, any purely decorative vases or ornaments can be displayed to give your home office a decorative touch. Arrange the items on show with care otherwise they will begin to look untidy and lose their appeal. Anything that is essential but unattractive is best stored out of sight. However, there are always some items that you need regularly and you will need to find a way to have them close at hand but well displayed. Do not have too many on open shelves, as it is more restful on the eye to leave some areas plain. These areas can be plain walls or a roller blind, but could equally be closed cup-board doors or shelving covered with panels.

Small storage items

Divide office essentials into boxes and baskets to make your work space more organized.

Small drawers will keep paper and compliment slips to hand. Computer disk boxes will keep disks clean and accessible. Baskets and fabric-covered boxes will give a tactile touch to the room but are a practical way of keeping small bottles, envelopes and string together and tidy. Tie on parcel labels so you know what is in each con-tainer. Fabrics stored in clear boxes or glass jars will show through and look decorative.

Practical points

As far as possible, all surfaces in your home office should be durable and easy-care so that they can take the inevitable knocks and wear. Melamine and varnished surfaces can be wiped clean, as can modern wooden furniture with protective finishes. Avoid anything that needs special cleaning as it will either cost a fortune to keep in pristine condition or soon look drab. For example, waxed furniture looks wonderful but spills cannot be wiped with a damp cloth; drycleanable fabric cannot be cleaned quickly enough to prevent marks setting in.

Flooring

Generally a smooth floor is the best choice in an office as spills can be quickly cleaned up and it is easy to dust and vacuum. The most economical wooden floor is to use existing floorboards and either sand and stain or paint them. They need to be in fairly good condition to do this, with no woodworm damage or nails standing up, and with not too many gaps or uneven areas. However paint is very good at disguising imperfections, especially if you paint on a design such as a chequerboard. Finish it with several coats of varnish to make it hardwearing. A new wooden floor will make a wonderful base for your room if you can afford it. Solid wood is very expensive but wood planks made

Chapter eight

Decorative details

T he surfaces you choose for your home office should be practical. Deciding upon the best finishes will make the space serviceable, longlasting and good looking.

with a veneer of wood under a thick protective layer look very good. Laminated wood-effect floorboards are more affordable and look nearly as good as the real thing. Vinyl tiles or sheet

Above: A good-looking office can be practical and hardwearing with light wood floor, plain walls and large windows.

flooring is easy to clean and extremely hardwearing.

In a room that gets light use as an office, a carpet can be used. It would be better to choose a low-pile carpet as anything else will flatten, especially if you have a chair with castors.

Windows

To keep the look of the room neat, it is best to avoid lavish window treatments. By all means hang curtains from a pole but keep them simple, perhaps plain and light in colour, and preferably washable. However, if the window is close to the desk or the room is small, a blind is a better choice. Ready-made roller blinds can be cut to size and are available in many colours. Venetian blinds in wood or metal will filter the light into the room and look orderly. If you like fabric, a pull-up Roman blind will add softness but still have an air of neatness, as it is contained within the window surround. Light colours at the window will help make the most of available light and filter it rather than blocking it out. In a sunny room, it is a good idea to have some kind of blind or sheer curtain to filter out bright light.

Safety

Computers are an important part of our everyday lives now, for work and pleasure, and if you

Walls

Paint is the least expensive and most durable surface for walls. Matt vinyl emulsion has an attractive chalky finish but vinyl silk with its slight sheen is easier to wipe clean. Around the desk you could fit tongue-and-groove panelling painted in eggshell or gloss for a more durable finish. If you prefer wallcovering, a vinyl finish will be more hardwearing than wallpaper.

plan to spend a lot of time at a screen it is essential to take precautions to avoid eye strain, backache or even crippling repetitive strain injury. Make sure the screen is positioned so that your eyes are level with the top of it, directly in front of you, at a distance of 50 cm (20 in) to 70 cm (28 in). The work surface should be high enough to allow your legs to fit underneath comfortably and for your forearms to rest on it horizontally. There should be enough space on the front edge of the desk to rest your wrists.

When planning your office remember that light should not shine directly onto the screen to cause reflection or glare, or come from behind it. A good position is close to a window to make use of the natural source and at right angles to it, so the

light is coming from the side. The chair you use should support your back in an upright position, with an adjustable seat to support your thighs in a horizontal or slightly sloping downwards position. Your feet should be flat on the floor and if you are short you may need a footrest – you could use a telephone directory.

If you do a lot of copy typing, use a vertical paper holder positioned close to the screen.

Take plenty of breaks from the screen. Stand up and do something else so that you do not overtire arms, back and fingers from constant, small repetitive movements. Your eyes will also benefit from a change of focus.

With all the electrical equipment in today's offices, there are bound to be plenty of trailing flexes. The best solution is to have extra power points fitted where the equipment will be positioned and, wherever you can, wind up the flexes and either hang them from the wall or tape them to the underside of furniture so that there is no danger of tripping.

From time to time, check that the leads, wire and cables as well as the plugs are not damaged in any way. Turn off electrical equipment at the power point at the end of the day if practical.

Planning your lighting

Good lighting allows you to work safely without risk of any eyestrain or headaches and will create a pleasant atmosphere in the room. The lighting plan is one of the most important considerations in a home office and, if at all possible, it should be decided before you decorate.

Once you have planned where the pieces of furniture will be placed, you can decide on the position of the light fittings. If you are to have ceiling spotlights, place them so that they are not behind you when you sit at the desk – or you will be sitting in your own shadow. It is better to move them so that they are alongside the desk or right over it. Spotlights should also be fitted in front of bookshelves or cupboards. If you have a seating area, a power point for a tablelamp will be needed nearby so that you can read comfortably. New power points, wall fittings and repositioned ceiling fittings will make all the difference to the lighting and atmosphere of the room.

Types of light and how to position them

The most basic type of lighting is general or background light. This could simply be an enclosed ceiling light that gives a source of light so you can see to get across the room. All rooms need this as a backup to

Chapter nine

Lighting

For any tasks involving close work, good lighting is essential. A successful arrangement should combine a bright source for the work in hand with pleasant background lighting. Storage space needs to be brightly lit, without too much contrast between areas of light and shade.

other specific lighting qualities, but ceiling spotlights fulfil this function while serving a second, more useful role. Background light could also be provided by uplighters that wash the wall with light or by a table or floor-lamp, with a shade that creates a soft, diffused glow.

A direct source of light is needed for working and a desklamp is perfect. Nothing beats the adjustable swing arm style, which gives a directional pool of light that will extend and move to precisely the spot where you need it. If desk space is limited, it could be wall mounted or clipped onto a nearby shelf. Always place lamps on the opposite side to your working hand so that shadows do not fall on your work.

Accent lighting can be purely decorative, to highlight a favourite object, or be a useful pool of light on a bookshelf or cupboard. Ceiling or wall-fixed spotlights will do the job nicely.

Above: A desk should be positioned close to a window so there is plenty of natural light. An adjustable desk lamp, or even two, is essential to light the work in hand.

If you want a good, clean light, look for fittings that use halogen bulbs. They are usually low voltage, so the fitting stays cool and the bulb is long-lasting. This may be the best light if you are matching colours regularly.

A dimmer switch will give a more controllable and adaptable source of overall light.

Chapter ten

Children's study areas

Right: Where space is in short supply, a desk can be squeezed in by thinking vertically. Here a high-level bed leaves plenty of space underneath for a study area.

C hildren like to have space that they can call their own – and a play and study area is a good idea if space allows. As with the adult's home office, this may need to share space with another room. A child's bedroom can be split into two – a dedicated work area should encourage the child to paint, write or even finish homework in their own special retreat.

Designating an area

A separate room would be ideal and a study/playroom can be adapted from an old utility room or garage – if it has not already been claimed as an adult's home office. More usually, a study area needs to be designated in the child's bedroom. As with adult home offices, it is best if it is sectioned off a little so that toys and games do not distract when homework needs to be done. Place a desk and chair in the corner of the room with an openwork screen painted in a jolly colour to separate it from the rest of the room. Or an open bookshelf can be positioned at right angles to the wall to make a separate study zone, but natural light from a window should be nearby.

Useful furniture

A desk and a chair are obvious starting points, but something inexpensive can be chosen for a small child so that it can be replaced as the child gets bigger. Later on, an adjustable desk chair on castors can be raised as the child grows, as can a desk made from adjustable trestles with a piece of wood as the work surface.

Unprepared wood furniture is an inexpensive way to furnish a child's bedroom and can easily be repainted over the years.

Colourful boxes can be used as storage for paper, pencils and paints and placed on a bookshelf for easy access.

A large noticeboard above the desk can display paintings and favourite pictures.

Style

A child's study area should tie in with the rest of the bedroom, whether this is colourful and bold or pretty and pastel. As with an adult's study, it is best not to make the area over fussy, as it will be difficult to concentrate in a muddle of patterns.

Storage

Shelves filled with storage crates are the easy answer to children's clutter. These can be divided again into small boxes for small pieces and labelled or colour coded so you know at a glance what is inside.

Boxes can be stacked on shelves alongside books. Small books can also be put away in big boxes. Toys need to be close at hand, so tall cupboards and high shelves are not a good idea.

Adapting as the child grows up

Plain walls that can be given a new coat of paint are the most adaptable. Borders can be applied and the walls painted over more easily than scraping off old wallpaper. Keep to bold, bright colours and change curtains and blinds.

Look out for furniture that adapts and grows with the child. High-level beds often have desks underneath that will come into service as the years go by.

Project one

Storage unit on castors

This neat triangular shelving unit will hold plenty of stationery. It can be wheeled out while you work and turned to face the wall at the end of the day so that all the clutter is hidden.

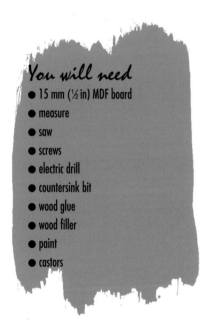

You will need

- 15 mm (½ in) MDF board
- measure
- saw
- screws
- electric drill
- countersink bit
- wood glue
- wood filler
- paint
- castors

1 Cut out the following from MDF: one square piece, 60 x 60 cm (23½ x 23½ in) for the back; one triangle 60 x 43 x 43 cm (23½ x 17 x 17 in) for the base; 58.5 x 30 cm (23 x 12 in) for the central divide; and two triangles 29 x 29 x 41.5 cm (11½ x 11½ x 16¼ in) for the shelves.

2 Mark the centre of the base triangle so you have the position of the central vertical divide. Join the vertical divide to the base by drilling two holes and fixing with screws from the underside of the base. Saw off front point of base.

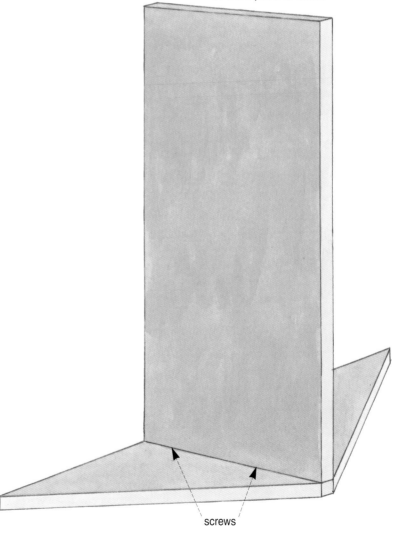

screws

3 Screw the base and the central divide to the back so that the base is in line with lower edge of the back. Mark the position of the shelves by drawing a line across the back and either side of the central divide, 30 cm (12 in) from the top.

5 Take the second shelf and apply glue along one 29 cm (11½ in) edge. This will be the edge that fixes to the central divide. Screw the other 29 cm (11½ in) edge through from the back. To secure the shelf fix a screw diagonally near the front.

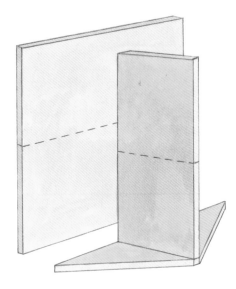

4 Fix the first shelf to the central divide and the back with screws fixed through the back and the central divide.

final screw

6 Fill screw holes and paint. Fix castors to each corner.

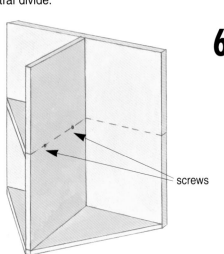

screws

Tip countersink screws so that when they are screwed in they are just below the surface. First drill a narrow hole to get you started. Use a countersink bit on the electric drill to cut a sloping side at the top of the hole. Drill a pilot hole less than the screw length, then fix in screw.

Tip choose castors according to your floor. There are different ones for hard floors or carpet.

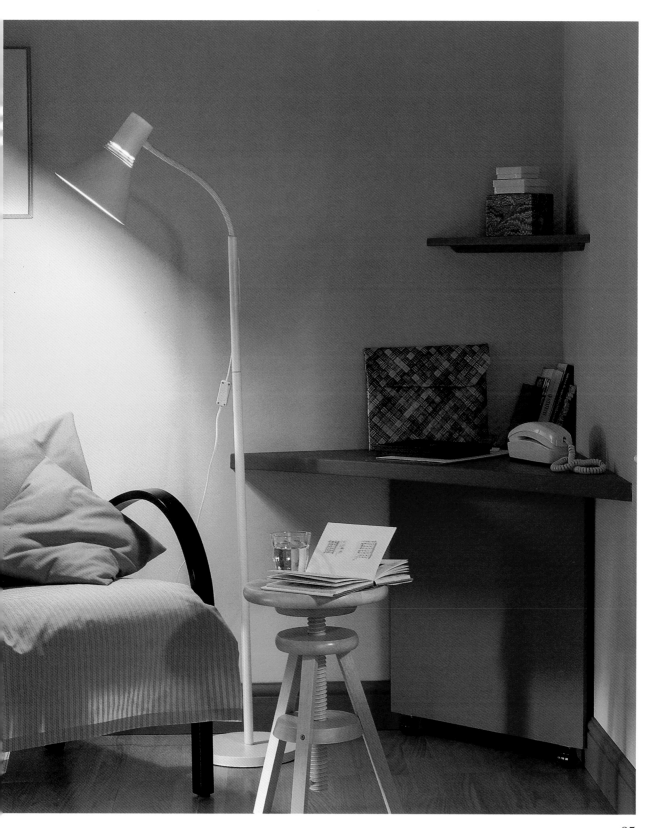

Project two

Pencil pot and floppy disk box

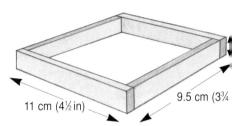

11 cm (4½ in)   9.5 cm (3¾

A n everyday item such as a tin can is ideal for turning into a
pencil pot. For something in which to store your floppy disks,
you could either recycle an old gift box or make your own box.
Decorate both pot and box with stamps linked by colour or by
subject – such as animals or flowers.

3 Select stamps that look good
together. Stick the stamps to the
box overlapping the edges slightly so
the box is completely covered.

You will need

- food can with the top cleanly removed
- firm card
- masking tape
- craft knife
- measure
- pencil
- PVA glue
- burnt umber paint
- stamps

1 Cut out pieces of card for the
box and lid.

For the sides you will need two
pieces 10.5 x 10 cm (4¼ x 4 in) and
two pieces 8.5 x 10 cm (3¾ x 4 in).
For the base, one piece 10.5 x 9 cm
(4¼ x 3½ in).

For the lid, one piece 11 x 9.5 cm
(4½ x 3¾ in), 2 pieces 11 x 2 cm
(4½ x ¾ in) and two pieces 9 x 2 cm
(3½ x ¾ in).

2 To assemble the box, place the
ends of the 8.5 cm (3¼ in) wide
pieces against the 10.5 cm (4¼ in)
wide pieces, so that you have
right-angled corners. Stick together
with tape. Place on top of the base
and cut away any excess. This will
depend on the thickness of your
card. Tape the sides to the base.

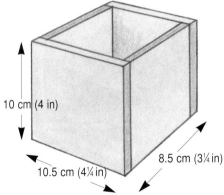

10 cm (4 in)

10.5 cm (4¼ in)   8.5 cm (3¼ in)

Make the lid in the same way,
taping the 9.5 cm (3¾ in) side
pieces just inside the 11 cm (4½ in)
side pieces. Tape together. Tape the
top of the lid to the sides.

● Optional idea as shown on the
can, right: dilute burnt umber paint
in water and paint over the surface
to give an aged appearance.

4 When dry, dilute the PVA glue
and paint over the surface once
or twice to give a protective finish.

Tip ready-made boxes
are available in wood or
card from several mail-order
craft suppliers.

Project three

Updating a metal filing cabinet

Old metal filing cabinets are quite easy to find in secondhand shops but are usually in drab colours. A colourful new look can be made with spray paint and decorative lettering.

You will need

- steel wool
- metal primer
- spray/aerosol paint
- small pot of white gloss or enamel paint
- outline of lettering
- tracing paper
- soft pencil
- masking tape
- white gloss or enamel paint
- artist's paintbrush

1 Remove drawers. Clean and prepare all the surfaces. Rub away any rusty areas and apply primer to any exposed metal.

2 Spray the frame white and the drawers in contrasting colours. Follow the instructions on the spray can. Shake it thoroughly, then hold the can about 30 cm (12 in) from the surface and use a long sweeping action so that the paint covers smoothly. Leave to dry and then repeat until completely covered.

3 Enlarge your chosen lettering from a book or page 63 using a photocopier. Use the tracing paper to trace around the outline of the lettering. Turn the tracing paper over so the reverse side is uppermost and carefully draw around the outline once more.

4 With the lettering reading correctly, tape the tracing paper to the middle of the drawer and trace around the lettering so the outline is transferred onto the drawer. Carefully handpaint the letters.

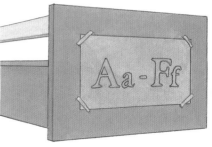

Tip check the instructions on the spray can as some metal paints do not require a primer.

Tip it is best to do this job in a garage or workshop with good ventilation. Protect the floor with newspaper.

Project four

Wallfile with three pockets

This handy wall-hung file will keep notes and stationery close to hand. It is made from rectangular pieces of plywood hinged at the base of each pocket and held with ribbon. Adapt the size to suit A4 paper or cards and envelopes.

1 You will need plywood: one piece 70 x 35 cm (27½ x 13¾ in) for the back; three pieces 21 x 35 cm (8¼ x 13¾ in) for the holders.

2 Draw out the shape and then score along the lines using a metal ruler and a craft knife. This will prevent the wood from splintering. Cut out with a saw and lightly sand any rough areas.

3 On each of the small pieces of plywood, make a mark 1.5 cm (½ in) from the side and 6 cm (2¼ in) from the top, on either side. Drill a hole through these marks.

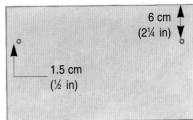

6 cm (2¼ in)

1.5 cm (½ in)

4 Paint each piece of plywood with one or two coats of wood wash or coloured varnish.

35 cm (13¾ in)

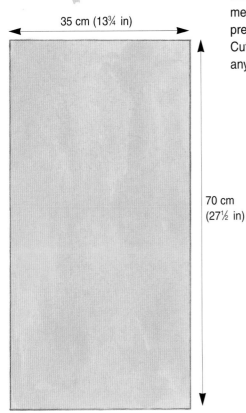

70 cm (27½ in)

35 cm (13¾ in)

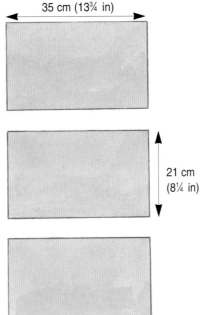

21 cm (8¼ in)

5 Attach a length of piano hinge to the lower edge of each of the small pieces so that the hinge edge is in line with the edge of the wood.

6 Place one small piece on the bottom of the back piece so that it is in alignment and screw together (above). Attach the remaining two pieces so that there is a gap of 1 cm (½ in) between pockets (below).

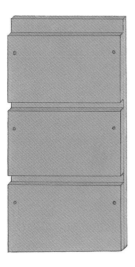

7 Make a mark through the drilled holes onto the back. Through each pair of holes thread a 60 cm (23½ in) length of ribbon and glue neatly to the face of the back using the marks as guides. Fold the ribbon lightly where it will meet the back and apply glue to this point. There should be a space of about 10 cm (4 in) from the top edge of the holder to the back, when the wallfile is hanging vertically. Lay flat while the glue dries. Fix picture rings and wire to the back and hang.

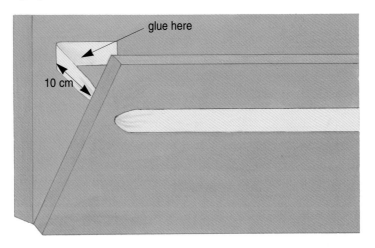

glue here

10 cm

Variation

A similar wallfile can be made with corrugated plastic card. The overall size here is about 60 x 24 cm (23½ x 9½ in), with the front pieces each 15 x 24 cm (6 x 9½ in). The card is attached to the back with a strip of strong reinforced tape instead of a hinge. It works in just the same way as the card is so light. The holes are made with a single hole punch and gift wrapping cord threaded through to hold each pocket and to make a hanging string.

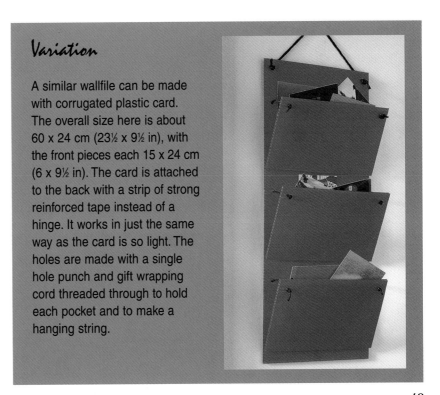

Project five

Screen to hide the work area

A screen is a clever way to hide a small area such as a desk. It is an excellent movable divide that acts as a temporary wall to section off the desk from the bedroom and can be moved to open up the desk when needed. Pockets on the desk side of the screen make extra storage and keep small items handy.

You will need

- ready-made MDF screen or three pieces of MDF about 185 x 50 cm (73 x 19¾ in), either shaped at the top or straight
- nine hinges
- small screws
- 4 m (4½ yd) light wadding
- small scissors
- dressmaking scissors
- 4 m (4½ yd) of 122 cm (48 in) or wider plain fabric
- 5 m (5½ yd) of 122 cm (48 in) or wider gingham fabric
- staple gun
- bradawl
- upholstery pins
- hammer covered with wad of fabric
- about 14 m (15 yd) of 1 cm (½ in) wide braid
- PVA glue

1 For the plain side of the screen. Cut three pieces of wadding to the size of the panels and staple gun to one side of each. Trim off excess.

2 Cut three pieces of plain fabric to the size of the panels, here about 185 x 50 cm (73 x 19¾ in), plus 5 cm (2 in) on each side. Lay the first piece over a wadded section of the screen. Make sure the fabric

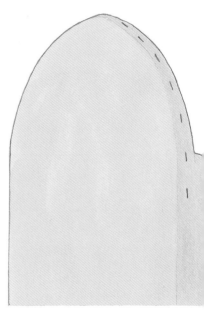

runs straight and central and fix with a couple of staples at the top. Fix the staples parallel to the edge of the screen and centrally in the thickness. Leave a gap of about 3 cm (1½ in) between staples. Follow the shape around either side of the top, pulling the fabric so that it is taut but not twisted out of shape. Fix at the bottom to keep the fabric straight and staple along the remaining sides, folding under the corners neatly where necessary. Trim away the excess fabric.

3 Cut the fabric for the opposite sides. For the two outside panels where there is one pocket you will need fabric 225 x 60 cm (88½ x 23½ in); for the central panel with three pockets, a piece about 285 x 60 cm (112 x 23½ in). Fix at the top as before, then, where you want the pockets, fold back the fabric by about 15 cm (6 in) and staple in place. Staple in between the existing staples and trim away excess fabric.

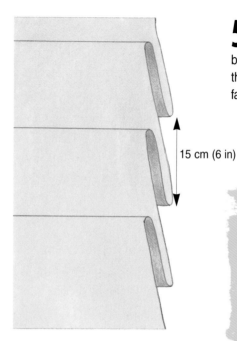

15 cm (6 in)

4 To fix the upholstery pins, make a mark close to the outer edges and in the centre of the upper folds of fabrics. Make a hole through the fabric and into the panel with a bradawl. Hammer in upholstery pins.

5 Join the panels together with the hinges. Then, starting at the bottom of the panel, glue braid along the edge to hide the staples and fabric edges.

Tip cover the hammer with a few thicknesses of fabric to prevent the upholstery pins from being damaged as they are hammered in.

Tip attach small castors to make the screen easier to move around the room.

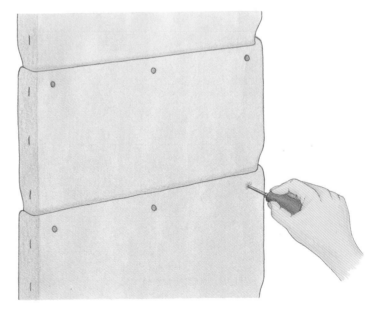

Project six

Noticeboard with clips

No matter how much we abandon paper in favour of the computer, there will always be notes, receipts and cards that we need to keep close at hand. This decorative noticeboard will store them all neatly and attractively.

1 Cut out the insulation board to the required size. Cut the angled decorative wood moulding to fit around it, mitring the corners.

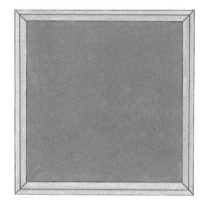

2 Cut the felt to the same size as the board and glue it to the surface of the board with PVA glue.

3 Paint nameplates, bulldog clips, cuphooks and moulding with enamel paint. When the moulding is dry, fix around board with glue and tacks. Retouch paint as necessary.

4 Stick rick-rack to inside edge of the moulding with PVA glue, pushing the middle well into the join.

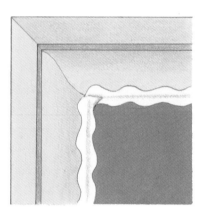

5 At regular intervals, fix screws on which to hang bulldog clips and screw nameplates above each one. Screw in cup hooks along lower edge of the board. Fix picture frame rings to back and wire for hanging.

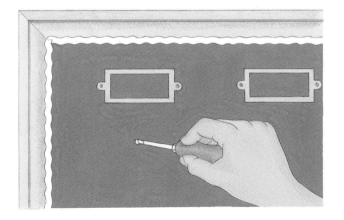

You will need

- 12 mm (½in) insulation board
- angled decorative wood moulding
- mitre block and saw
- felt
- PVA glue
- wood glue and tacks
- nameplates
- short screws
- bulldog clips
- cuphooks
- enamel paint
- rick-rack tape
- picture frame rings and wire

Project seven

Bureau

A neat fold-away desk is created between two shelves in an alcove. The lower shelf is hinged to make an extended work surface that folds up to close. This produces a plain panel to decorate as you wish. Here it has a freehand design inspired by the Bloomsbury style.

● For an alcove of 30 x 90 cm (12 x 35½ in), the sizes are:

Two shelves 28 x 90 cm (11 x 35½ in), extension flap 30 x 90 cm (12 x 35½ in). Flap-support holders in 6 mm (¼ in) MDF to measure 5 x 27 cm (2 x 10½ in) and four pieces of 12 mm (½ in) MDF to measure 2 x 27 cm (¾ x 10½ in).

Two pull-out supports in 19 x 25 mm (¾ x 1 in) batten, 28 cm (11 in) long.

Shelf batten supports in 25 x 25 mm (1 x 1 in) wood, two 90 cm (35½ in) long, and four at 22.5 cm (9 in).

1 Using a spirit level, mark the height of the desk shelf and then another shelf 28 cm (11 in) above. Screw the battens along the back wall and then to both side walls.

2 To assemble the support holder, use glue and tacks to attach the 12 mm-thick (½ in) MDF lengths along the edges of the 5 x 27 cm (2 x 10½ in) piece of 6 mm (¼ in) MDF (above, right).

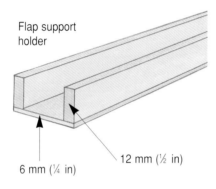

Flap support holder

6 mm (¼ in)   12 mm (½ in)

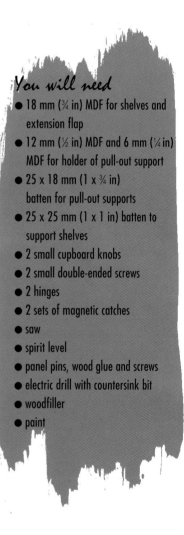
3 About 4.5 cm (1¾ in) from each side of one shelf and level with the back edge, screw the support holders through the depth of its side pieces into the base of the shelf.

4.5 cm (1¾ in)   4.5 cm (1¾ in)

27 cm (10½ in)

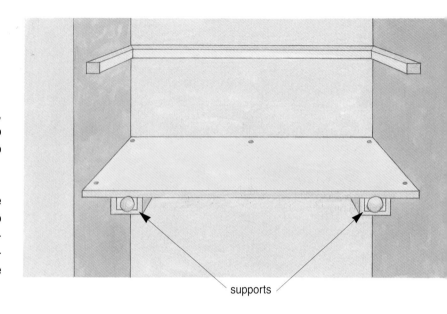

supports

4 Using double-ended screws, attach the cupboard knobs to the end of the supports and slot into the holders.

5 To fix the lower shelf onto the batten, screw from the top into the batten. Countersink the screw-heads so that they lie below the surface of the wood. Repeat with the shelf above.

6 Attach the 30 x 90 cm (12 x 35½ in) piece of MDF to the front edge of the lower shelf with two sets of hinges. When closed it will line up with the top of the upper shelf and be flush with the wall alongside. Fix two sets of magnets to the face of the extension flap and the edge of the upper shelf.

7 Finally, fill the screw holes and paint. You can be as creative as you like when decorating the front of the panel.

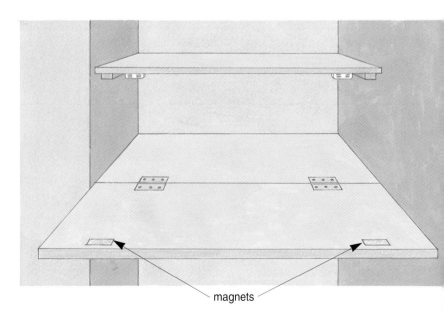

magnets

Project eight

Panel to cover open shelves

O pen shelves make excellent storage, but can look fussy and distracting if filled with lots of untidy things. A fabric panel will hide everything neatly from sight.

You will need
- cotton fabrics
- backing fabric
- thread
- sewing machine
- touch-and-close tape

● Seam allowance is 1.5 cm (½ in) throughout

1 Measure up the front of the shelf unit and add on 1 cm (½ in) to the width so that it covers fully. For a 62 x 102 cm (25 x 41 in) panel, we used 30 13 x 13 cm (5 x 5 in) squares in yellow and 30 13 x 13 cm (5 x 5 in) squares in magenta. For the edging, you need two pieces, 4 x 64 cm (1½ x 25 in) and two pieces 4 x 104 cm (1½ x 41 in). For the backing fabric, you need one piece, 65 x 105 cm (26 x 42 in).

2 With right sides together, pin and tack a row of fabric squares up to the width of the required panel. Alternate the fabric colours and start half the strips with yellow and half with magenta. Sew the squares together. Open the seams and press down neatly.

3 Keeping the pattern correct, pin, tack and sew the strips together to make the panel. Open seams and press down neatly again.

5 With right sides together pin, tack and sew the backing to the patchwork front, leaving a gap of about 25 cm (10 in) along one side so that you can turn the panel through to the right side. Trim seams to 1 cm (¼ in), turn through and press. Hand sew to close the opening.

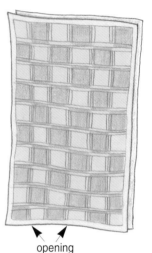

opening

6 Top stitch around the panel 1 cm (¼ in) from the edge to give stability (below). Sew touch-and-close to the top edge of the panel.

7 Stick sticky side of touch-and-close to the top front of shelf and press panel in place.

4 With right sides together and edges level, pin and tack the longest pieces of edging to the sides. Stitch together. Trim seams to 1 cm (¼ in).

Open up and press along the stitch line. Repeat the process with the two shorter edges.

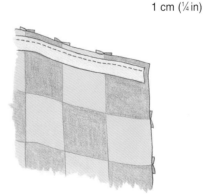

1 cm (¼ in)

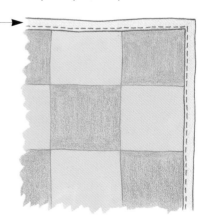

You will need

- four wooden storage boxes
- a piece of MDF, 50 x 150 cm (20 x 60 in)
- woodwash in white and blue
- paintbrush
- measure and pencil
- masking tape
- satin-finish wood varnish
- electric drill
- small screws

Project nine

Desk on boxes

All you need for a desk is a good-size work surface at the right height. Storage boxes are a quick way to make a desk base.

1 Paint the insides and outsides of the storage boxes with white woodwash. Leave to dry and repeat once or twice more until the colour is quite dense.

2 On the outside, divide the sides with handles into three equal strips. Draw light pencil lines and edge with masking tape (below). Paint the outer parts in blue woodwash. Repeat until the colour is as strong as you wish.

Tip be sure to measure the boxes before you start so you have a desk that is the right height. If it is a little low, add feet made by cutting blocks from a 45 x 45 mm (1¾ x 1¾ in) length of wood.

Tip trestles are a good starting point for a desk, cut down to the right height if necessary. A flush-panelled door can be used as a work surface. Crates or metal containers will also make good bases – in fact, anything that stacks and is steady and strong can be used.

Tip trestles can be bought from specialist furniture stores with ready-made table tops. A piece of toughened glass would also serve as a table top.

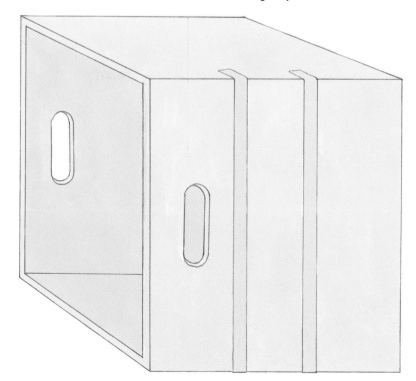

3 Make sure the MDF work surface is clean and apply a coat of varnish. Reapply two or three more times to give it a hardwearing finish. Sand surface lightly between coats.

4 Screw the two sets of boxes together, with screws at each of the inside corners (right).

5 Turn the work surface upside down and place the boxes at either end, about 20 cm (8 in) from the front of the desk. Fix the work surface with screws through from the top of the boxes into the underside of the work surface (below).

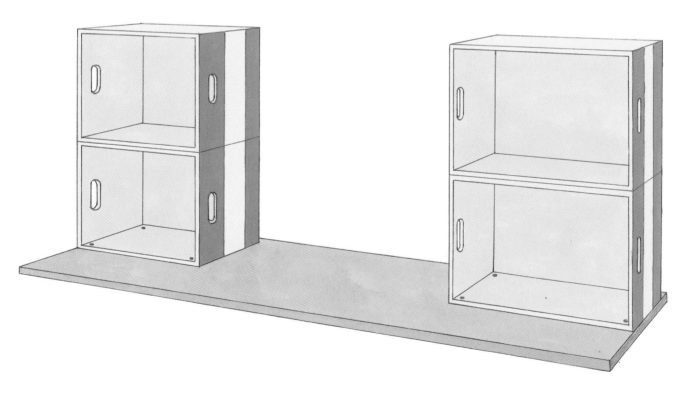

Project ten

Child's fold-away desk

A tiny fold-down desk makes a temporary desk or play place in a room with little space. The hinged surface is held open with lengths of cord, and hooks hold it closed.

1 Using a pair of compasses draw out 10 cm (4 in) scallops around three sides of the MDF boards. Start at the corners. Draw a line 5 cm (2 in) from the edges to help you draw them straight, then work along the lines. Cut out with a jigsaw. In one piece, draw and cut out a central 7.5 cm (3 in) heart shape.

2 Drill one 2 cm (¾ in) in diameter hole within the second scallop on both sides of both pieces of board to hold the cord.

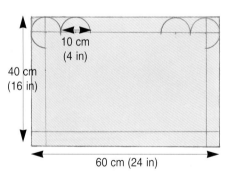

3 Paint with primer and then two coats of eggshell paint. Join the two pieces of board together with the hinges.

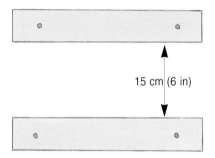

15 cm (6 in)

4 Decide on the height of the desk and the back board. Fix the two lengths of batten to the wall with screws, horizontally and about 15 cm (6 in) apart (above).

5 Screw the board with the heart in it to the battens with the screws. Countersink the screws so that they are below the surface level and can be filled and painted over.

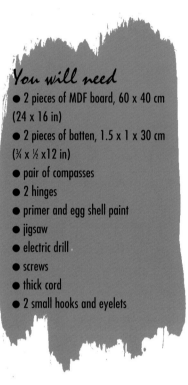

6 Thread lengths of cord through the two holes on the back board and tie firm knots. Thread through the holes in the work surface and tie knots to hold it level. Screw in two eyelets at the top of the back board and attach hooks to work surface to secure it in a closed position.

Lettering

If you are updating an old metal filing cabinet (see project three, on page 38) take this page to a photocopying shop and ask them to enlarge the letters to the size you need. If you prefer, you could choose your lettering from a book or magazine and have that enlarged instead.

Aa-Ff
Gg-Mm
Nn-Ss
Tt-Zz

Acknowledgements

Plasti-Kote
Sawton, Cambridge CB2 4TR
01223 836400
Super Enamel and Odds 'N' Ends in Night Blue,
Country Blue, Turquoise and Teal, page 39

Victoria Carpets
Green Street, Kidderminster, Worcestershire DY10 1HL
01562 823400
Carpet, page 45

Dorma
PO Box 7, Lees Street, Swinton, Manchester M27 6DB
0161 251 4400
Sophia bedlinen, page 45

Shaker
27 Harcourt Street, London W1H 1DT
0171 724 7672
Desk, chair and bin, page 45

Coloroll
Riverside Mills, Crawford Street, Nelson,
Lancs BB9 7QT
01282 617777
Chair, page 51

Cuprinol
Adderwell, Frome, Somerset BA11 1NL
01373 465151
Wild Blueberry and White Ash Woodwash, page 59

John Wilman
Heasandford Industrial Estate,
Widow Hill Road, Burnley,
Lancs BB10 2TJ
0800 581984
Wallpaper, Toile Stripe 450092, page 61

With special thanks to Roscoe Interiors, Stephen Gott
and Naomi Purkiss.

Index